BACKYARD ANIMALS
COTTONTAIL RABBITS
by Kristin Petrie

Checkerboard
Library

An Imprint of Abdo Publishing
www.abdopublishing.com

www.abdopublishing.com

Published by Abdo Publishing, a division of ABDO, PO Box 398166, Minneapolis, Minnesota 55439.
Copyright © 2015 by Abdo Consulting Group, Inc. International copyrights reserved in all countries. No part of this book may be reproduced in any form without written permission from the publisher. Checkerboard Library™ is a trademark and logo of Abdo Publishing.

Printed in the United States of America, North Mankato, Minnesota.
102014
012015

THIS BOOK CONTAINS
RECYCLED MATERIALS

Cover Photos: iStockphoto
Interior Photos: Alamy p. 15; Corbis pp. 20–21; Glow Images p. 7; iStockphoto pp. 1, 11; Jim Brandenburg/Minden
      Pictures p. 7; JOEL SARTORE/National Geographic Creative p. 29; Justin Russo / Solent News / Rex Features For
      more information visit http://www.rexfeatures.com/stacklink/CJPZNCPJD (Rex Features via AP Images) pp. 26,
      27; Science Source pp. 5, 7, 12, 13, 16, 19, 23, 25

Series Coordinator: Megan M. Gunderson
Editor: Tamara L. Britton
Art Direction: Neil Klinepier

Library of Congress Cataloging-in-Publication Data
Petrie, Kristin, 1970- author.
  Cottontail rabbits / Kristin Petrie.
      pages cm. -- (Backyard animals)
  Audience: Ages 8-12.
  Includes index.
  ISBN 978-1-62403-659-0
1. Cottontails--Juvenile literature. 2. Rabbits--Juvenile literature. I. Title.
  QL737.L32P48 2015
  599.32'4--dc23
                          2014024348

TABLE OF CONTENTS

RABBITS!

Rabbits. Some are fun, lovable pets. Children and adults adore their innocent eyes, twitchy noses, and velvety fur. They can have long, floppy ears and cute, cottony tails.

Other people despise rabbits! Gardeners, farmers, and homeowners curse these furry creatures. Rabbits devour garden vegetables and profitable crops. They munch on flowers, shrubs, and other backyard treats.

Pets or pests, all rabbits belong to one big scientific family. This is the family Leporidae. The family also includes the rabbit's relative, the hare. The family Leporidae is divided into more than 10 groups called **genera**. Cottontail rabbits make up the genus *Sylvilagus*. Welcome or not, they are a common sight in many backyards in the United States, Canada, and beyond.

SCIENTIFIC CLASSIFICATION
Kingdom: Animalia
Phylum: Chordata
Class: Mammalia
Order: Lagomorpha
Family: Leporidae
Genus: *Sylvilagus*

CONFUSING NAMES
A Belgian hare is a type of rabbit. A jackrabbit is a type of hare!

Members of the family Leporidae are found on every continent except Antarctica.

COTTONTAIL RABBITS

The genus *Sylvilagus* is divided yet again into types, or species, of cottontail rabbits. There are more than a dozen species of cottontail rabbits found in North and South America. Several of these live in the United States and Canada.

Many cottontail species have common names reflecting the **habitat** in which they live. The swamp rabbit, *Sylvilagus aquaticus*, lives in wetlands and swampy areas. *Sylvilagus audubonii* is the desert cottontail. It inhabits dry areas of southwestern North America. The mountain cottontail, *Sylvilagus nuttallii*, lives in the western United States in areas around the Rocky Mountains.

One of the most common cottontail rabbits is *Sylvilagus floridanus*, or the eastern cottontail. This species thrives in many regions, climates, and habitats. It is a familiar sight in gardens, fields, and of course, backyards!

A swamp rabbit

A desert cottontail

An eastern cottontail

A mountain cottontail

7

HABITATS & HOMES

Where do cottontail rabbits live? Just about everywhere! Cottontail rabbits are found from Canada to northern South America. In the United States, they make their homes from the East Coast to the Great Plains. They are also found in the West.

Cottontail rabbits are widespread due to their ability to adapt to almost any **environment**. This includes extreme regions such as deserts and rain forests. Some species need very little water. Others survive on whatever food is present. What about areas with cold weather? Cottontails grow a thick coat to stay warm.

Within their regions, cottontails prefer to make their homes on the edge of wooded areas next to open areas such as meadows and farmland. They are found in fields, prairies, marshes, and swamps. They prefer to have bushes or tall grasses because these areas provide cover. The cottontail also seeks easy access to food.

SPECIAL TALENTS
Unlike most rabbits, the mountain cottontail climbs trees! It walks up sloping tree trunks and drinks dew from the leaves.

Canada

United States

Mexico

SOUTH AMERICA

N

■ Where Cottontail Rabbits Live

North America

Europe

Asia

Africa

South America

Australia

9

TWITCHY NOSE TO COTTONTAIL

Cottontails of all species are similar in appearance. They have full, egg-shaped bodies and long, powerful hind legs. Their eyes are large and their ears are long. And of course, they have the short, fluffy tails that gave them their name!

Within the same species, males and females do not look different. Their fur color and body shape is the same. However, females may be slightly larger.

Species differ from one another mainly in size and color. The swamp cottontail is large. It can weigh nearly 6 pounds (2.7 kg) and measure almost 22 inches (56 cm) long! Eastern cottontail rabbits are smaller. They weigh approximately 2 to 4 pounds (0.9 to 1.8 kg) and are 15 to 18 inches (38 to 45 cm) long.

The cottontail's back legs and feet are long. These feet are also furry on the bottom. The toes on all four feet end in long claws that are slightly curved.

GIRL & BOY NAMES
Male rabbits are called bucks.
Females are called does.

THE COTTONTAIL RABBIT

EARS

EYE

NOSE

FOOT

TAIL

The cottontail has a soft, double-layered coat. As a mammal, it is warm-blooded. Its dense undercoat helps it stay warm. The outer coat is coarse and varies in color.

Many species have black, brown, or gray-tipped **guard hairs** covering the back. Others vary from red to white. The cottontail's underside is white. This color extends to the tail. This gives the appearance of a cotton ball when the rabbit is on the move.

The eastern cottontail's coat has a brownish undercoat with black and gray-tipped guard hairs. This mixed coloring serves as excellent camouflage in its surroundings.

THE EARS HAVE IT!

A cottontail's ears can help you figure out what species it is. The desert cottontail has black-tipped ears. The brush rabbit has no fur inside its ears, but the mountain cottontail's ears are lined with white fur. The New England cottontail has a black spot between its ears.

The white underside of the eastern cottontail's fluffy tail shows when the rabbit is running. It also shows when the rabbit is relaxing!

The Appalachian cottontail looks similar. However, its ears are shorter and rounder and feature black edging. And, there is a black spot between them.

Cottontail rabbits that live in cold climates **molt** two times per year. Spring molts produce a lighter-weight coat for warm weather. The spring coat may be a different color to match the cottontail's **habitat**.

Fall molts leave heavier, warmer coats for cold weather. These molts may also result in color changes. For example, eastern cottontails develop longer, more gray-colored fur. This helps them blend into snowy surroundings.

NIBBLING ON PLANTS

What do rabbits eat? Carrots, of course! Cottontail rabbits also eat a variety of other foods. They are herbivores, so their diet consists of plants only.

Plants still provide a lot of variety for the cottontail. In summer months, the cottontail munches on many green plants, such as clover, herbs, and wild grasses. These rabbits also are well known for their love of garden vegetables. This includes beans, peas, and lettuce. Fruits such as apples and strawberries are a part of the cottontail's healthy diet as well.

Most of the delicious foods of summer are unavailable through the winter months. During this time, the cottontail nibbles on hard materials such as bark and twigs. Buds from maple, oak, and other trees also round out the winter diet.

Contrary to popular belief, cottontail rabbits do not nibble all day long. They are crepuscular (krih-PUHS-kyuh-luhr), which means they do most of their feasting at dawn and dusk.

TIME TO REST

During the day, cottontails spend their time in a shallow cavity called a form.

The cottontail's diet varies by season.

Rabbits get most of their water from the plants they eat. They also drink from pools of water when available.

Digestion of the cottontail's high-fiber diet starts in the mouth. First, the rabbit uses its sharp **incisors** to slice plant food into sections. These sections are pushed back to the molars. These back teeth smash tough food into small pieces. The cottontail's teeth grow year round to keep up with this hard work.

The cottontail's mushy meal travels into the stomach for further breakdown. Next stop is the intestines. The rabbit's digestive system has a lot of work to do with those tough food sources!

Some of this tough matter is **excreted** as little round droppings. Other matter moves to a special pouch called the **cecum**. There, the food is further digested. This food matter is then expelled in softer globs. Do you dare guess what happens next? The rabbit eats it!

As gross as that sounds, rabbits really do eat their waste. This is a process called coprophagy (kuh-PRAH-fuh-jee). This gives rabbits another chance at valuable nutrients. They are absorbed when these droppings pass through the digestive system a second time.

EXTRA TEETH?
A rabbit's four top incisors come in two pairs. One sits directly behind the other!

BABY RABBITS

Cottontail rabbits are well known for their rapid reproduction. Why? Rabbits begin breeding when they are very young. Both male and female cottontails can reproduce just two to three months after their own birth! In addition, females can reproduce up to 7 times per year! Four **litters** per year is most common.

However, reproduction is highly dependent on a few factors. For example, climate, food availability, and **photoperiod** all affect the eastern cottontail. With ideal conditions, its mating season runs from February to September.

The female cottontail is **pregnant** for 26 to 30 days. A few days before giving birth, she digs a nest. She lines it with soft fur pulled from her belly as well as grass. These nests are hidden beneath logs or shrubs or in areas with tall grasses. The male cottontail does not help with the young.

A mother rabbit covers the nest with fur and grass. This helps keep her young warm as well as safe from predators.

It may seem strange that the mother only visits her young once or twice a day. However, this may help draw less attention from predators.

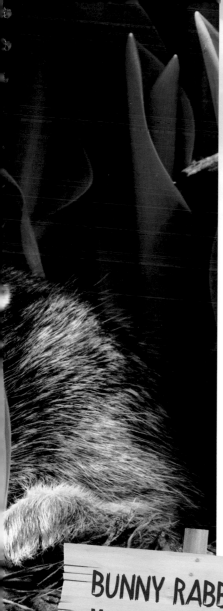

The mother cottontail gives birth to 1 to 12 kittens, or kits. The average **litter** size is 3 to 5. Cottontail newborns are tiny! They weigh just 0.9 to 1.2 ounces (25 to 30 g) and measure only 1.2 to 2.0 inches (3 to 5 cm). They are also blind and helpless.

Despite a newborn's helpless state, a mother cottontail provides very little care to her young. However, she does nurse her young. This happens one to two times per day. These feedings help the young rabbits grow very quickly.

The newborns' eyes open between days four and five. At two weeks of age, they have grown, have fur, and are ready to roam. Despite their growth, the young rabbits are not yet independent. They still return home to nurse. The mother cottontail **weans** her young by a few weeks of age. Usually, she is ready to birth another litter by this time!

Littermates become tired of one another by this time, anyway. It is a good time to spread out. Plus, many will begin breeding shortly.

BUNNY RABBITS!

Many people use the word bunny to refer to young rabbits. Scientists call baby rabbits kittens, or kits.

BEHAVIOR

Rabbits are solitary by nature. They do not like to hang out together, but they do share territories. The cottontail's home range is generally five to eight acres (2 to 3 ha). The male's range is slightly larger than the female's. Home ranges increase in size during breeding season.

You might see a cottontail hop into a backyard during the daytime. However, these rabbits are mainly crepuscular and nocturnal, or active at night. Daylight hours are wisely spent hidden beneath logs, shrubs, or other cover. During this time, the cottontail naps and grooms itself.

Rabbits also periodically stand on their hind legs with their forepaws tucked to their chests. In this position, they watch for predators or other rabbits.

Cottontails venture out of their hiding spots at dusk. Nighttime activity starts with a feeding. Rabbits continue to **forage** throughout the night. Dawn signals more feeding and then a return to shelter.

CROWDED HOME?

Up to 8 to 10 eastern cottontails can live in just 2.5 acres (1 ha).

A cottontail grooms itself to keep its fur tidy. It uses its front paws to groom its face. It licks its body and legs, bites its feet clean, and scratches its sides with its long back feet.

COMMUNICATION

Cottontail rabbits use numerous forms of communication. Mating calls include squealing, while distress calls are in the form of shrill cries. Cottontails also cry out to distract predators or warn other rabbits of danger. This is especially true of mothers with nests.

Excellent senses of smell, vision, and hearing also help the cottontail avoid danger. Large, rotating ears catch sound from all directions. Big, round eyes are on either side of the head. This means rabbits can see better to each side and behind than they can to the front. It helps them watch for predators.

The cottontail's twitchy nose has a sharp sense of smell. Rabbits know other rabbits by their scent. They use scent glands to mark territory and pass on information. Perhaps most important, this keen sense of smell detects predators.

The cottontail's many communications and its excellent vision, hearing, and sense of smell are essential to survival. Still, due to its many predators and vulnerable size, most cottontail rabbits do not live longer than three years.

Rabbits can rotate both ears at once or just one at a time.

ENEMIES & DEFENSES

Cottontail rabbits have a large number of predators. These include ground-dwelling creatures such as snakes, weasels, coyotes, and foxes. From above, they risk the claws of hawks and owls.

Trying to be invisible to predators is the cottontail's first defense. Like many other animals, its coat blends into its **environment**. This natural camouflage and the cottontail's ability to freeze in place keep predators from spotting them.

Cottontail rabbits can also slink away from danger. When slinking, the cottontail lays its ears close to its head. It crouches low to the ground and slowly moves away from peril.

BOING!
An eastern cottontail can leap 15 feet (5 m) when zigzagging to escape a predator!

With a predator chasing it, the rabbit relies on flushing. This involves rapid, unpredictable movement in a zigzag pattern toward a place of shelter. When freezing, slinking, and flushing fail to work, the rabbit uses speed to escape. Rabbits are fast! They can reach 18 miles per hour (29 km/h).

Humans may be the cottontail's greatest predator. Humans hunt rabbits for food, **pelts**, and sport. In addition, the growth of urban areas destroys the rabbit's natural **habitat**. And, rabbits are at risk from vehicles.

Zigzagging and leaping helps break up any scent trail a rabbit might leave behind. This makes it harder for predators to follow it.

STRONG POPULATION

People may harm a rabbit's **habitat**, but rabbits may also have a negative impact on a people's habitats. In its natural search for food, the cottontail consumes profitable vegetables and crops. In its search for shelter, it damages lawns and other intentional landscapes.

The cottontail's rapid reproduction often means increased damage in these ways. In addition, some rabbits carry bacterial disease such as tularemia, or rabbit fever. Disease can pass to people who touch dead rabbits.

On the other hand, cottontail and other rabbits are beneficial for their fur, meat, and role in the ecosystem. Due to their reproduction and ability to adapt, most cottontail rabbit populations are strong and stable. The **IUCN** lists a few species as vulnerable, near threatened, or endangered. Yet most are considered least concern, with some populations increasing!

Even in the coldest winter weather, cottontails do not hibernate.

GLOSSARY

cecum (SEE-kuhm) - a part of the digestive system after the small intestine and at the beginning of the large intestine.

digestion - the process of breaking down food into simpler substances the body can absorb.

environment - all the surroundings that affect the growth and well-being of a living thing.

excrete - to pass waste material out of the body.

forage - to search.

genera - more than one genus. A genus is a group that scientists use to classify similar plants or animals. It ranks above a species and below a family.

guard hair - one of the long, coarse hairs that protects a mammal's undercoat.

habitat - a place where a living thing is naturally found.

incisor (ihn-SEYE-zuhr) - a front tooth, usually adapted for cutting.

IUCN - the International Union for Conservation of Nature. The IUCN is a global environmental organization focused on conservation.

litter - all of the babies born at one time to a mother rabbit.

molt - to shed skin, hair, or feathers and replace with new growth.

pelt - an animal skin with the fur still attached.

photoperiod - the length of day, which affects the growth and behavior of plants and animals.

pregnant - having one or more babies growing within the body.

wean - to accustom an animal to eating food other than its mother's milk.

WEBSITES

To learn more about Backyard Animals, visit **booklinks.abdopublishing.com**. These links are routinely monitored and updated to provide the most current information available.

INDEX